THE DISORDERED ALPHABET

THE DISORDERED ALPHABET

POEMS

CINTIA SANTANA

FOUR WAY BOOKS
TRIBECA

LIBRARY OF CONGRESS CATALOGING-IN-PUBLICATION DATA

Names: Santana, Cintia, author.

Title: The disordered alphabet / Cintia Santana.

Description: New York : Four Way Books, [2023]

Identifiers: LCCN 2023004455 (print) | LCCN 2023004456 (ebook) | ISBN
  9781954245624 (trade paperback) | ISBN 9781954245631 (ebook)

Subjects: LCGFT: Poetry.

Classification: LCC PS3619.A568 D57 2023 (print) | LCC PS3619.A568
  (ebook) | DDC 811/.6--dc23/eng/20230210

LC record available at https://lccn.loc.gov/2023004455

LC ebook record available at https://lccn.loc.gov/2023004456

This book is manufactured in the United States of America and printed on acid-free paper.

Four Way Books is a not-for-profit literary press. We are grateful for the assistance
we receive from individual donors, public arts agencies, and private foundations
including the NEA, NEA Cares, Literary Arts Emergency Fund, and the
New York State Council on the Arts, a state agency.

We are a proud member of the Community of Literary Magazines and Presses.

for

Estrella Torres Gutiérrez (1921–2005)

and

Félix Sastre Uría (1921–2011)

and for Hideo

beside me every step of the way

CONTENTS

Notes

We came to the broken place and went through it.

William Faulkner, *The Sound and the Fury*

Word

Widsith spoke, unlocked
their wordhoard, they who
sent upon us wellcloud of
wordpour, abundance — we
who were made to grow out
of the earth and return to it;
so in the six-hundredth year
of our life, in the second
month, on the seventeenth
day of the month, the
windows and the fountains
above the great deep broke
open at once and the words
rained down upon us for
forty days and forty nights,
which is to say much, but in
the words that we used then.
What was the matter with us
that we did not fear such
breaking? What became of
all that we did not say with
those words before new—
fallen ones washed them
away? The world as in the
beginning become wild and

waste, the face of words not
separate, and then separate;
words from words as, too,
the waters from the waters.
And all the while the runic
wynn changing to ruin. Even
as she-dove showed us a
well and therein the we, and
a mouth breathed out a pale
blue moth, and from the
whorl of a whelk a newborn
elk stepped impossibly out,
blinking. All the earth was
made wet and webbed-wide,
a well and a wellspring, a
worden, the sluices of
heaven wording as we
stood in that great rushing
wind within, yet without
name, turning.

Qaṣīda of Grief

Desert sand I am.
A ruin, a dull desire
so I desire the said: O.
Oasis. Estuary. Oxbow.
Dawn. I donate my dead.

Crow. Caw. Bare.
Crow. Caw. O. Awe
at these losses in the desert.

You. Humid. Hewn.
My moon meadow.
My brass door. Glass.
Ash. My elder.

Cuerpo. Cuervo.
Sorrow. Sew.

So.
This is newness.
O.
Upper pasture.
Hay hidden under snow.

Notes to a Funeral

1. According to the old law, the body must be buried within two days.
2. Lit so that nothing looks like it's under glass. As in a museum.
3. Compare "Those are pearls that were his eyes" (*The Tempest*, I. ii. 398).
4. That is, despair, carrion comfort, feasts on her.
5. A narrow passage between houses or, as here, rocks.
6. The imperative, "Take," while understood here, does not appear until the next stanza.
7. Originally, a dialogue in verse between two shepherds.
8. Rice paddy. River and shrine. Rain (Jpn.). The recalled imagery contrasts with the growing threat of snow.
9. Alludes to the scene in which the princess writes a letter and gives it to the page. The page sets off but cannot find the temple; he longs for the familiar capital.
10. "In the end, you, too, will complete your assignment and, like me, return to the capital."
11. *Nine Ways to Cross a River*, 2008, 179.
12. Suite, famous for its intimate sarabande, the second of only four movements without chords. Tortelier describes it as an extension of silence.
13. The imprint of his body in the grass.
14. A memory that unfastens.
15. The full phrase asks, "Is man but a parable for God?"
16. "We obey but we do not comply" (Sp.). Maxim with which the Guipuzkoans vetoed the laws of the Spanish sovereign.
17. *Language as Gesture*, 1952, 352.
18. Devotions, performed in memory.
19. *Collected Poems (1921–2011).*
20. ". . . swallowtails lift from the railway tie" (*Letters*, 120).

Apple

Adam

        is dreaming

          of a bomb

     Atom

        become

            A-bomb

            A-bomb

            So many

     atoms

            in this

            @

The Hand that Lifts the Latch Lifts the Bird at Last from Its Battered Cage

Nobody remembers the fluorescence of that night
nor the voices of the desert traveled by his breath

Madrid, December
the oxygen turned high as it will go

In the street, ribbons of people
tie and untie, prepare for the coming of kings

Mercy of a kind is morphine
a foil-covered drip, the eye of God that's shown

welcome to the blue

hour, welcome to the final
destination, the body's home
address, there are rooms here
you will never want to know
but now you know: glass-
paned and built in shade of
shipyard, someone else at the
prow, oh god, you say, oh
god, by which you mean your
daughter's name —dial it
down now, yes, you hear me,
dial it down; the wattage of
the world turned up, all knives
in sharp relief, how once you
were attached to her and now,
now this, the plating of the
head, red barn is being razed;
hard to find fresh flowers on
a grave —sweeping, so much
sweeping —east house is
down.

[E=]

we the once
> that are

were and will be
> how we long to see

the wild apple
> the lizard's bright blue throat

to say
> *spring*

sakura
> to say

again

we the once
> that are

were and will be
> did not expect— I crossed
>> aioi bridge on bike
> a stone in my pocket
>> for sharpening knives

every wristwatch
      stopped
8:15
      enola
his mother's name

           above hijiyama hill
             I saw the splitting of the light
         their elijah
            carried skyward
         in a chariot of fire

our lips
      sealed into scar
each throat
      an open grave

the current was faster than I thought
when my feet touched bottom
I thought I had reached the other side

I was found
my bento
under my body

I was not found

we waited for fine gauze
to bandage our eyes
around and around

I, so unlike a butterfly
watched
the skin of my hands peel

at night
      red clouds
as if woven from raw silk

                      I called out for water
                           but there was no one to hear

then from the skies
      that sealed our city's fate

                  black rain

we drank

in november
      beside the burned grove of bamboo
a canna bloomed

                    my mother found
                      my wooden sandal

Want

Mother, I am plowing by moonlight
I am without word or water
The sorrel mare went without fight
Mother, I am plowing by moonlight
In this pigweed world, sown through with flight
What profit from this blood? What daughter?
Mother, I am plowing by moonlight
I am without word or water

Dear N

No map for this,

                my love.

No chart.

                No stars.

Death takes

                before

it takes again.

Midnight, Barking Desert

In the hollow of the hollow tree
In the night's night and the deep ravine
The world's awhirl when I look up

More is misnomer than we know
More is more seed than can be sown
I keel and cobble, I reel, I keen

And all the deities are made of stone
And a widow, young, cannot give up her rings

Ringing: the world is ringing
There's fever in the eye
I'm driving mirrors through the night

Dear Mr. Vastness, Dear Mr. School

The lessons are getting harder.
Although I have studied, I feel no more prepared.

The switchgrass.
The shadow on shale.

The white of birches so like the white of skulls
—is that what is meant by voice?

I know to sing through woods
but I did not anticipate the need for knives.

The river is without banks.
The red thread around my wrist has snapped.

Morning: empty corral.
Undress me.

At Forty I Dream of Home

Unbuilt, or charred to this, the timbers of my house, its ribs. Alone, but
standing, it whistles wind into the bluestem grass. A structure on a lot,
a shape I could—or did—call home.

On the front lawn, but nowhere to be found, the small mound
I called a hill. The dwarf juniper. The white stone lantern. The markers
of my childhood yard have not been planted yet nor laid.

Or perhaps the yard has changed hands. Many by now, altered by each.
The chokecherry ravaged by the indifference of strangers. Only the dirt
remains.

Time of my mother's cancer, the third or fourth. Time of the guests
to impress. Drawers crammed with silver; every tine tarnished.
Impeccably behaved, I ache for a dog, a boat.

I am walking by it now, with a lover from long ago (do I build again?
at all? at first? I will not pass this way again). I am walking now.
I am waking now.

Throughout the day, locked inside a white tile bathroom, I revisit
the strange blooms of my blood. My dog keeps dying. I save
her and she dies again.

Grief, Summer

after Tomas Tranströmer

Once there was a death
that left behind a plain pine box of ashes.
It could not keep her inside. She lingered
around every corner in the house; the air
gathered, shaped itself into the pale heat of her form.

I can still go to the farmer's market
on a summer solstice day. Peel back the ears
of corn to check for worms startled by the sudden
light. The farmer knows them inoffensive
and will eat a rejected cob at day's end.

It is still beautiful to travel level to the clouds.
It is still beautiful to watch a man in a long-tailed boat
cast a butterfly net into the swiftness of the Mekong;
the human speck is still to scale. But the human hive
has grown louder. And home is a nest made of wax.

Dear N

I have never been

           this North.

No Eden, this.

           No East.

I am tender

           to the touch

but there is no touch.

Portrait of a Marriage as
Library after Air Raid, London, 1940

1.
Luck has left
the tidy shelves of books intact

and a leaded window in the back,

each square divided
into smaller, beveled panes. *Defy,*

they say. *Survive, survive.*

2.
Three men in bowler hats
stand before the shelves and browse.

As if oblivious to the ruins of the house,

the terrors of the previous night, they study spines,
reflect. Wear woolen overcoats amidst the char.

A timber holds the standing walls apart.

3.

Under rubble, a ladder and a covered chair, crushed.
The archive, leather-bound and made to last.

What once was roof reveals the vastness
of the sky. Inside becomes outside.

Everywhere, the shock of light.

II

I am your wild

your lash and your
sword, runaway
orbit, your transom
in the night. Stop-clock
and gird, manifest ache,
I've got the teeth. I'm
your top, your spin, your
early spring; lover
of the world's small
welts and the hornworm,
I will only live on weather
-ward shore. Tremble
and sway, guy-wire,
ruby-hued stalk, your
shroud and your stay.
City cured by fire, dark
between stars, sash,
exhale, and splash: I spill.
I am barn to the yard,
mane to your horse.
Behold my face, I'm torn
awake, I take my fill.
When no one else will,
I'll shoot the dog.

Dear T

From under my wing
          they are taken.

First my father,
          then my firstborn.

Take it, the world
          tells me.

How I want to leave it.
          Take it,

the world says.
          On the chin.

Again.
          In stride.

Back, I say,
          take my breath.

Dear T

Before I was alive,
      Trinity.

The target,
      a T-shaped bridge.

Then towers, two.
      Everything twice:

a sword edge,
      faced.

Someone takes the train.
      Someone else,

the bullet. Towns, entire,
      too, are taken.

In the wind, the twist,
          the fate.

The knife, in my
          twisted arm, twisting.

Cloven tongues
          like those of fire.

In the teapot, a tempest,
          thief-thick.

Dear U

under the water, the tow,
        the taking; upwind.

and under the taking,
        the story untold.

you, for whom this is written,
        unbidden, you bid me.

unwritten, unuttered, you wrote,
        you spoke me.

and so, with no choice, I rose,
        a voice, competing with a bell.

and so I stand here before you,
        before the wild carrot's umbel,

its small umbrella of ribs;
        and so I stand here before you

and say to you, for whom this is written,
        understand that in the beginning

I asked for nothing.
          untangle my hair,

unbutton, unmake me;
          I do not flinch.

Dear C

Can't. I can't. You
can. And do. You
cut. You seize. So
let me cease. I want
to close. I want you
close. Openly, I crave:
May. What come. Oh,
there are curves. There
are culls. Call it circum-
stance. *Condemno*;
Roman letter of
sadness. Caesar, my
Caesar, cut my cord.
Still my breath
then carry me.

Dear Y

Yes I will, yes I say, my voice break free;
raise, braid, combine, these yowls, these
disparate why's, that keel, that quake, that
drum me. I *am*—am *something*: days, years

yet to come. Yet choose—yes—yet, to be. Yet awe,
yet owe, be yawed. Why will you not an open wound
let be? Why yoke the yearling? Hew the redbay?
My midnight in the desert hallowed will not be.

That to this world I might yet wake? To hyssop,
quaking aspen, red-crowned crane? Which when
the main vein of sadness forks, insist, remain?

World is yucca flower, consonant and vowel,
union split into little splits, branching. Oh, wind
-born sake, I ash, I live oak, bending, yield.

Welter

On the eighth day, we had nothing left to write.
The dry land had begun to grow wet again.
We could call back our image no more
than we could call back the river, the rain.
With matters in this way, we decided to go.
But we hovered over the waters.
Shored the blue-black vault.

Shōwa. A Monday. Clear skies.
The knowledge in our jaw traveled,
lodged itself into a knot behind our ear.
Already we could see the roof tiles bubble,
the sandstone head of Buddha peel.
We thought of the zero, the one, and the why.
But we go for broke; we horse-carry.

We wrote some more.

R Writes Me a Letter

So I
was born.
From Resh.
Then a-
gain from
P. One
day, one
more leg.
A tent
-ative
tenta
-cle inched
forth. Touched
ground.

There are
no rules.
A rasp
become
berry.
Bid be
-come bird.
The thrill
of a
trill, the

r's rol

-ling. And

yet. Ray,

radi

-ant, ra

-dia

-tion. Or

-bit re

-duced to

obit.

Railroad

ties I

have seen

burst in

-to flames.

Entire

cities

turned to

rubble,

to ash

reduced.

Hush now.

Shh. There

is no
rush. No
rake that
rips out
root. Turn
ice in
-to rice.
Your road
to ode.

The Soul Speaks to the Body,
the Body Being Hurricane, Barrier, and Gate

Gale
    and gust, must
you insist again? By just
    such truths storms break booms. Slam. Retreat.
Brought by water, returned by water.

Stone
    walls dare land
-fall. Surge. Wreckage. Blue hour bears
    down now. Switches. Power lines, lash,
submerge in salt. Will it do then to

dry
    them out or,
better yet, tunnel deeper?
    Restore the power. Restore the
sun. Unrip the roof. Run, trains, again,

run.
    I make no
mistake; your crooked course aims
    straight for me. I am harbor, sea
gate under siege. Raise me the waters.
    Batter me, I am path.

Inherit

In her, it.
It, in her.
Heredi-
tary she

heard it said.
Or somewhere
read. Her hair.
Her thinning

hair. Her hear-
ing, poor. Her
heir. She was.
In her was

her. In there.
The air a-
round her, her
air also.

Mother. Moth
to light. To
air. She, too.
She. Two.

Self-Portrait in Available Light

I lived in the available light.
Taken by moonlight during a fire.
A newborn grief, not a minute old.
My place in the night-album.
A memory without a mirror.

What shall I say about the shadows?
And all they revealed to me?
The blue light and the door ajar.
The mother, hidden, to still the child.

Tip the light and the eye will follow.
The small, spinning lamp in the corner, gleeful.
A cigarette's ember near center.

I, all of these, belonged to someone once.
The Kremlin under snow.

The photographer unknown.

Self-Portrait as the Letter *I*

Improvise.

[D]

I found a Dictionary in my Dream,
A Book so like a Door,
And knocking—knocking—soon I found
Each Word was hardly Worn—

The words defined and seated,
A Choir, black and white—
Kept singing—singing—till I saw
The Ink of Night divide—

I looked up Death, the DMV,
Saw Net to Nest unfold,
With those same letters, Roman, changed,
The Words—began to toll,

As all the Pages were a Bell,
And Being, but an Ear,
And I, unspeaking, some strange State,
Heard silence—veer—

And then all Sense in Letters spoke
And language detonate—
And every Word a World contained
And meaning to be—Made—

Elegy

Leather like a shoe, this
rat but flat, paper-thin
this had-been rat I'd pass
on wooded path from car
to gym. Always there, for
weeks—never moved—
until one day was gone,
blown, swept, brushed,
turned to dust, I don't
know, I only know it once
was a rat and I could tell
from the strand of small
bones it once swung as a
tail. Hail to the dead, to
my faithful, flattened star,
to the life whose life for
me began when it had
ceased.

Mr. Vastness and Mr. School Answer My Letter

Bhikkhus, the Buddha is said to have said, everything is burning

the soft hair on seeds
snow and the adjectives around you

Out of the depths we have called you

attempting to explain *wall*
may translate as *traitor* or *spy*

And the one who died in the river

be not deceived, Sister of Lazarus,
by silence, spring of speech

There are so many ways to ache

and the forms of fire, these, too, are many:
how the box of ideal mirrors contains light

We call back the sun, the salmon, the flame

and in the absence of matter, the void, too, is affected
and over each a prayer said

every object in motion
every object at rest

Elegy for a Bell

] after
] and toward
] say this
] but going know
                      ] the good

] now riven

] no knell
] no tailor to the hours
] open sea[m]
]
]

loose me] if only I
] if there be
] wake
] call the   ] from the field
] stay my

] under glass dome
] the built world
] shard-bright

                    ] how thorough] the ruin

] my winter garden
]
all s[ave]
[s]wept
]
] I
] held
]

Dear T

The windmills
    are everywhere.

I tilt. I do not talk.
    My tongue taken,

I still find ways;
    I take horns

by the bull.
    Icebergs

and tip them.
    Third is the degree,

the rail. And time,
    slow charm.

I tick.
    I tock.

My blind eyes
    turn seeing.

My deaf ears,
    singing.

Let there be

light you said. And there was light. And there was lack.
Let there be life you said. And it was lush with loss.

Let there be lion and there was lion. There was lamb.
Let lion and lamb be divided, luna moth from moon. And it was so.

Let there be laughter you said. And there was laughter. Lap and lick.
Loin and purr. Lip. Loop. Leash—there was law. There was lynch. *Látigo. Luftwaffe.*

Land and labor. Lather and lathe. Leave, longing, lesson. Yes, there was lesson, too.
And lesser. And least. Loam and leaf. Load, ligature, and lie. There was lie.

Lapse. And lake. Luck and leap. Little by little. Letter by letter. And it was late.
And there was bloom.

Dear O

Out of the box, the frying pan, the gate running,
      I won this life on the nod.
Odd it is to be
      or not be.

So I loosen the noose and
      think. How in the beginning was the eye, the spring, and then
the tear, the drop.
      How in the beginning was the little *"o!"*
that issued us forth, and yes,
      terminal, too.

O,

I am out of my mind
      and in the woods with grief;
the world is whacked
      and out of order.

Day it is and there is no moon
      to be over.
I am on the ropes, the rocks, the razor's edge.

Over and over
　　　I say your name;
I breathe you in.
　　　Mouth without voice,
you circle round.
　　　1.3 billion light years away,
ago, two black holes collide;
　　　a bell in the universe
rings.

Ode to Your Salmon Soul

to your mother and your father / and their mothers and
their fathers / to the pale pink of their love / and their
cold / unseasoned waters / because they made / you
/ you / you / Ode to your mouth gasping / to its echo
of my gasping / to your bludgeoning / which is my
bludgeoning / and the tears lost to this water / Ode
to the bear's maw / wound-wide and lovely-dark /
To the quiver and muscle / the barb / the tidal marsh
and the cruelty of shallows / To the fight / the current /
the heave and the climb / to the higher / higher / heights
and the estuary's sky / a riot of stars / silent winks that
bind / Ode to the slope / the steepness / the leap and the
/ lope / To the feast / and the stones / to Chinook and
Chum / To the / sweet / eelgrass / to the first gravel
nest / and the next / To your / rings / narrow / wide / to
your hump / your growing / teeth and your / kype / Ode
to your / cherry skin / your darker / silver / blues to
your / milt your red / roe spilling / ripe / Ode / to you /
to / you to / you / to the / river rumoring / home

Kintsugi

in the art of *kintsugi* pottery is repaired by sprinkling powdered gold on lacquer
there is no attempt to hide the damage   the break is illuminated

I have been working in the olive groves   under a sky written by birds

late in the fifteenth century Shogun Ashikaga Yoshimasa sent a tea bowl
glazed in celadon   to China   for repairs

and in the iris of your eye   there is a storm that will not break

the bowl returned mended   crossed by a track of ugly metal staples

do you remember that April storm?   the river choked by wild onions?

we know little as to what followed   by the seventeenth century   collectors
valuable pottery   smashed   so as to be mended with gold

and on the river bank   the butterfly   folded

after mending   a piece can resemble only itself
the form determined   by the breakage suffered

every wintering knows its season   every bluethroat its flyway

the mouth brought to attention by interruption at three points

in the galleries of the body   the scapulae are paired
wide flat bones   the shape of wings

a pair of repaired scissors   too   brings tears to the eyes

again   today   I heard the rustling in the groves

Agaricales

Born a button under register of rain,
      Coaxed by the night bird, you dug
Deep into damp
      Ease of shade,
Flanked by ferns, your growth
      Groping forth blindly to fruit under the pine.

How did you come to be? Overnight
      I blinked and you sprung: gargantuan-lobed,
Jaundiced, trailing echoes of copper-colored
      Kin, some scallop-edged, all wet with swollen
Longing. Lobster you were not, nor lion's mane,
      Morel, destroying angel, stinkhorn—
None of these, of this I am sure if sure
      Of nothing but your order perhaps, and even that
—Poor guess—riddled by the oddities of your grammar, your growth
      Quelled by little.   How to

Read the syllabary of your skirt, make intelligible such
      Spongy syntax? Slick, expansive as meat and monstrous,
The mystery of your symmetry escapes me. An aberration
      Uttered into night, purloined from dirt and brought to ground,
Vowels grasping for height (were you one body or three?),
      World that was wood that is now word

expressed in you; tongue of earth's constant labor,
    You blister forth
Zero hour and speak.

[the atoms]

the atoms
coupling and
the taming
of the fire;
the vesper
sparrow and
the braided
bark; the green
kingfisher;
river, twice;

honeycomb
discarded
in the grass
raked by light;
reed-bed; birch
curl; the white
ibis; mouth
upon mouth;
the canyon's
lip, crumbling;

tethered to
this world is
all that I
love so let
me run my
wrists over
the diamond
tip of your
saw, salt-bloom
in my veins;

my eyes fill
with the trees,
the rain-bruised
fruit; atom,
simple seed,
scatters near,
vibrates on
the tongue, the
tumult of
the tongue, from
noise rises.

Voice

A
spruce
does not
speak
but for you
listening
to the borer—
—like a cork-
screw through
the bark—
—to the sound
made
each time
it hits
a new ring—
—a history to be
milled,
lathed
into pale
ribbons—
—released
through sound
holes in
the shape
of letters

or rosettes—

—a sound

that holds

the flick,

the fell,

the small

v the ax

delivers

to the trunk—

—for you I timber.

And riven

I river

through air

—vibrato—

the violence

in the violin

and the saplings

born to suffer

in my shadow

grow.

[K]

K had gone missing. I, J, L and M sat round the keyboard's open grave. A mouth gone mute. A white rubber eye left behind, blinded.

Perhaps on the plane. In the seat pocket in front of me no longer. In the hotel room—the rug—before the packing.

This had happened before: the Romans. After inventing G, they made C harder. K was all but converted. A rarity, a ruin. A Grecian hardness.

"K," I called and I called. No one answered. I looked for K's arm pointing skyward. The white rubber eye stared at me blankly.

In the dream, I plot with K against Queen Gertrude. We demand she issue a retraction. Given the circumstances, the Queen complies: "More art! Less matter!" K, my half-butterfly, winks at me; victory.

Some days I forget until I remember.

iss me ate. iss me.
K howls for a vowel.
Snowfall wakes me.

Quantum Khipu

;
not
Roman but
colored,
spun or plied,
cotton or
camelid, little
string mop
of talking
knots
burns
to the powers
of ten with
queer tales
of horses
for hens
; barley
and silver
; verses
; murder
; some sum
of multiple
milking
sheep
; I quake

at the heat

of the quick

-sprouted seed

; the littlest

leap

of the quark

flavored up,

down,

strange,

charmed

;

; quick

khipucamayu

; deliver me

; do not delay

the order

you offer

in witness

you hold

—so like an O

and yet—

Self-Portrait as Santa Ana: The General, the Saint, the Wind, and the Crypto-Jew

Something under the rug
      has been swept:
the wedding shot
      the gun; the thief
set out to catch another—
      but why? My spine
sends shivers down,
      and skin,
however saved,
      will not be bone.
So spring the chicken
      and sit the duck down.
Out, out!
      Undamn!
Sometimes
      there is no spot,
there is no time.
      The devil's winds are scattered
to the four,
      and from my eyes
fall all the scales.
      One thing is saying;
the other does.
      That moment in Saigon?

Old same, old same.

     The earth is saved

by salt and by a bell.

     So. I was not meant

to live on a shelf.

     Daylights scare

and the blood will sweat.

     But say it ain't:

the corrected self

     a rattling sabre,

a sacred something.

     Come,

be apple's sweetness.

     Tell me

the story of your name.

Wild!

Two trees and a question.

A red chicken in a partial frame—wild!

Bodies without organs.

A little mouth with little teeth. Nuns!

Not one. None!

Human reproduction on a copy machine.

Odor; three-sided

rhomboids; the social life of the page

—in several hands, all

of the seventeenth century. The hair at the back

of my head; the drum in your chest.

Bassoons. Baby baboons. Rain-trot

on roof. Libraries after dark

(—so wild!). Wigs. A forest full

of gongs gleaming; reading

in reverse. The slippery spot on a spotted floor.

The inventor of barbed wire. My love

and I, resisting rescue.

Notes to *X*

1. Alludes to the lyrics of a little-remembered song from the time:

   A kiss in a taxi

   attracts the horizontal axis.

   It marks the spot;

   it's practically por—no

   -graphic.

2. The colorful drawing in the manuscript's margin is of a four-horned sheep. While visually jarring at first, it has the merit of approximating the situation as we now have it, and of leaving open the unsolved question.

3. The image oscillates between birds darning the air and a coast live oak, uprooted.

4. The reader will immediately recall the scene in *Blade Runner* in which Deckard determines Rachel is a replicant and exclaims, "How can *it* not know what *it is?*"

5. Yes. Often.

6. "I have written a novel in which I have redacted each instance of the letter *x* using *the letter x!*" (Pierre Menard, personal communication).

7. Useful in this regard are the verses written by committee (but signed by Ezra Pound) (*Pound: Poems and Translations*, p. 1175).

8. Refers to the mixed reviews heaped upon the memoir, *I Was an Extra* (e.g. "Extraordinary!" *WSJ*, "Pretty extra." *NYT*).

9. *Crossing the Narrows, 1971*, p. 15.

10. What follows is a brief moment of complete darkness.

[H]

Held
heart
holed
whole.
Harpooned.
Heart on
but hard.
Hell
in a hand.
With harps.

Hark! I said.
Hear me.

Heart heard.

[Ear,
hear
heart
here.]

Heart's
a host
of hooves,

a horse
-drawn
hearse.

I wear it on.

Sonnet for My Hawk in G

God does
not darn.
He damns.

In Spanish,
you shit
on the sea

instead
of on God.
Gawd
is like

a hawk.
In you,
my hawk,
I believe.

[F]

First there was the sound
        of a serpent in the ear.
An angel
        falling
with a flaming sword.
        A fist. The use
of force.

Flood and fjord. Fog
        and foghorn. Flamingo,
flamenco, Flaubert.
        Frankenstein. Then Frisch.
Fission, then Fermi. Fascism.
        Anne Frank.
Flash, then fallout. The pamphlet
        from the Office of Defense:
To escape temporary blindness,
        bury your face in your arms.
To lessen your chances of injury by blast,
        fall flat on your face.

Little Boy.
       Fat Man.
Flesh
       of my flesh.
Sound of fat
       hitting fire.
Paper lanterns,
       drifting.

Fault and faultline. Fraud
       and fracking. The fracture
of a fact; a farm
       foreclosed.   Your face—
why forbidden?
       Grace, fastened
to an empty frame.
       Not forgotten; forgiven.
Fade as fate. Fat. Fa.
       Fados in the rain.

Hum

Slip of
bird with
fan
of furious
wings in
blossom's
throat I
hear your
wing
-beat sing.
To nectar
you need
no key,
mid-rib
of leaf or
sip from
little red
vials
constantly
defiled;
starvation
staved
for one
more day.
Butterfly

weed, too,

bids your

wing

-whistle

come:

sing me,

guard me,

lap me

with your

split

tongue.

Dear Z

Zero at the bone, I descend
       Your slender stem. Sharp, your angles,
X-treme your speed. Zorro wrote you
       With a sword, and versed you may be, but
Voiced? Tailed? Untailed? Zed, zeta or zee?
       Unhinge the door, the lid, the swinging parts.
Tip shadows slant and suture the white wake of my
       sorrow; why sting? Turn
roe into *rows* into *rose*, and having risen, radio this:
       —Quick, true story: zygote and zydeco
Paired up on the dance floor. Yoked, ever after.
       Oh, Oz was no wizard just an Omaha conman.
Nor does a word true what it names. See, my map never
       matched the terrain; the variations from a line,
Lick-sharp. My first kiss was in a darkroom.
       Knock and knot I have known.
Jazz and Jesus, too; in which to believe?
       I zig, I zag through places I have never been.
Haze with a chance of rain. Galaxies,
       Glass-made. There are people I have never known,
Forms that I will never take, never hammer, never hold.
       Ease me out when the time comes. My hair take beneath
Deep eaves for a taste of the wild leek. This is ground
       Control from Marble, Blue: unchart the stars forgotten by their maker.
Bless the zebra and the zander; the zabu and the keeper of the zoo;
       Alpha, Omega, Aleph and Zahir; the alphabet ends.

Ode to the J

Hey Jude, hey Judas, hey jumper on the bridge:
thirty pieces of silver buys you nothing
but a field of blood. And yet; how exquisite
it is to betray with a kiss. No sin is
original. No jail, a break. Blind, the river
and blind, the curve. Justice. Just north of July.
Silver-green June grass and bug right
beside you. See, Jacob was my brother,
and Jack, in the box that was my heart; but not
now. Blossoming reed, sprouting seed, a scoop
in the hand, a jujube tree. Jump shot
in a jumpsuit. A jingle and a jangle. Jungle
into gym into jumble. So tumble. We did
and we do. Jewel is to joule as jazz
is to truth. Oh, oh, the density of joy.
On a January jukebox. Stem no such flow.

Dear B

Never the bride.
Never been better.
Nor best. A burden

       is nothing like a bird.

A bus

      become a boy.

         Little Boy.

            A boy become a bomb.

Let bygones be.
Let bygones be.

Breath
    is but borrowed,

brief.

     And the body betrays

because you be:

burrow.

Bury

the black in the berry.

Bury

the bumble in the bee.

Bless the bean.
Bless the butter
and the cup.

Notes to the Name and Its Translations

1. The hammer of high wind. The editors recommend this pronunciation when reading aloud, but others may wish to follow their own custom (e.g. teacup clatter; rhythm of the rails; ring tone rising).

2. Historically, translations into English allude to a miniature person said to exist in the mind, with some exceptions, notably "Reading Whitman in the Grass."

3. This rendering, on doubtful grounds, introduces an overtly male emphasis through its constant use of "He." Compare with "You are the alpha and the asshole. The f'd up aleph."

4. "Too bad! Too bad!" (Ger.).

5. Some explanation is in order.

6. Not the palm but the shadow of the palm.

7. Every hair of thine. Euphemism fallen out of modern usage.

8. That is, an ideal mirror, lossless.

9. Orb of the eye; dark water. Perhaps a joke.

10. The fever underneath the hand.

11. Here, a loud knock on the roof at night. A later folio indicates the single toll of a bell.

12. Perpetual motion (Latin).

13. "So I go to the stranger's body and bend. I split my lip on the bone of his cheek and lick the salt from the spoon of his back. The day breaks behind his shoulder by shades. I sleep then and sleep and wake with him to eat" (*Selected Letters*, p. 28).

14. "You can learn more from the shadow than from the object itself" (*Military Counter Surveillance Manual*, Chapter 5, Lesson XXIII).

15. Blinded and thereby granted the gift of prophecy.

16. Triangular insert in the seam of a garment. Allows expansion.

17. Originally, a summer house. Here, by extension, the nationalist

movement, and even the whole façade of the temporal world. May also
suggest: needle and points on a compass; godwit, knot, rail, and ruff;
open pleasure-boats decorated with large swans that circulate on a pond
during summer months; the high-heeled boot worn by Greek actors
in tragedies, as well as the "sock" or light shoe worn in comedies; the
mariposa plum; a many-colored meadow; goat path; rainspout, flip-flops
in the rain; the forked root of the mandrake; the hum in the mouth; the
sweet cane.

18. All the while, the body, breathing.

19. Backlit.

20. In an interview, Del Berg, the last living volunteer of the Abraham
Lincoln Brigade, states, "It bothers me a little that at 99 you're going to
die any minute, because I have a lot of other things I want to do."

21. The extant fragment reads, "What I miss most about fishing is reading the
water."

m, anew

maybe the manatee
the mustard grass
and millet seed

maybe the matter
of mass, and what
it equals

a marvel, the moment
a minor terror
a mercy

a movement
in the manifold
held

as a madeleine
is to memory
mapped

in the mouth
and in the mind
your mouth

in my mind's
eye, inscribed
and having

made it
to the moon
I say

hello, moon
hello, darkness
hello, moth and mole and mountain

PLOSIVE

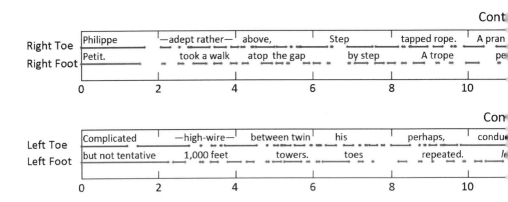

Cont

| Right Toe | Philippe | —adept rather— | above, | Step | tapped rope. | A pran |
| Right Foot | Petit. | took a walk | atop the gap | by step | A trope | pe |

0   2   4   6   8   10

Con

| Left Toe | Complicated | —high-wire— | between twin | his | perhaps, | condu |
| Left Foot | but not tentative | 1,000 feet | towers. | toes | repeated. | l |

0   2   4   6   8   10

State: Right Leg

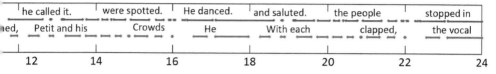

State: Left Leg

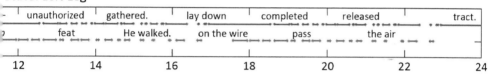

NOTES

QAṢĪDA OF GRIEF

The poem begins with a translation of the first line of Miguel Hernández's "Casida del sediento," followed by a homophonic translation of the Hernández poem.

[E =]

I visited the Hiroshima Peace Memorial Museum in August of 2013 and May of 2018. The images in the poem are inspired by these visits and by materials at the National Peace Museum and its online archives documenting the atomic bombings in Hiroshima and Nagasaki.

SELF-PORTRAIT IN AVAILABLE LIGHT

"Hidden mother" photography is a term for a practice common during the Victorian Era. Because long exposure times were required to register an image, a mother or caretaker was in the frame but hidden under fabric (e.g. curtains or upholstery) in order to hold children still for the photograph. See Linda Fregni Nagler's *The Hidden Mothers* (2013).

The term "night-album" stems from a critic's disparaging reaction to Louis Daguerre's claim that he had found a way to make permanent images created by light. The critic, Alphonse Eugène Hubert, wrote that such an image would require Daguerre to make a "night-album enclosing his results between black paper and only showing them by moonlight," in order to avoid their further darkening by continued exposure to light. See Kate Palmer Albers, *The Night Albums: Visibility and the Ephemeral Photograph* (2021).

[F]
The italiciced lines are taken from the booklet, *Survival under Atomic Attack*. Executive Office of the President. National Security Resources Board. Civil Defense Office. NSRB Doc. 130. United States Government Printing Office. Washington D.C. 1950.

NOTES TO THE NAME AND ITS TRANSLATIONS
Berg, Del. (As told to Dan Kaufman). "The Last Volunteer." *New York Times Magazine*, March 3, 2015. Web.

PLOSIVE
The graph represents a tap-dancer's motion as inspired by Ikegami Y., Ayusawa K., Nakamura Y. (2012). *Masters' Skill Explained by Visualization of Whole-Body Muscle Activity*. (In: Noda I., Ando N., Brugali D., Kuffner J.J. (eds). *Simulation, Modeling, and Programming for Autonomous Robots*. SIMPAR 2012. Springer, Berlin, Heidelberg. I have extended the original study's graph by four seconds.

ACKNOWLEDGMENTS

Grateful acknowledgment is made to the editors of the following publications in which these poems, sometimes in differing versions, first appeared:

Anti-Poetry, Beloit Poetry Journal, concīs, Conjunctions, Gulf Coast, Gulf Coast Online, Harvard Review, Interdisciplinary Studies in Literature and the Environment, Iron Horse Literary Review, Kenyon Review, Michigan Quarterly Review, Pleiades, Poetry Northwest, Rhino, Spillway, Sycamore Review, The Threepenny Review, and *West Branch.*

IN GRATITUDE

To my parents, Mariela and Jorge, who gave me the world and a love for language.

Rita Mae Reese: your workshop in the fall of 2007 awoke the poet in me who had been slumbering since high school.

Bruce Snider: fundamental. Thank you for your friendship and your considered, keen insights on craft and my nascent work.

Brittany Perham: you let me audit your class at what you didn't know was a very difficult time in my life. It was under such kindness that the first letter to a letter was born.

Genine Lentine! Your fierce intelligence and compassion over the years have led me down remarkable, unsuspected roads.

For David Baker: a teacher's teacher and the most generous of mentors. Your unfailing support and attention to my work continues to be a gift I cannot repay.

To all my poe' peeps, my OxyGente, my Poetry Palooza, my Tiny Workshop. To be among you is to belong.

To the Djerassi Resident Artists Program: for letting me take my poetry off the page and into the woods.

Brian Cochran: my comrade in the deepest trenches of poetry. Love; always.

To Jim von der Heydt: you poured your intelligence and attention on every word, punctuation mark, and white space I gave you to read; such generosity is a special kind of love.

Thank you: Ryan Murphy, Bridget Bell, adam bohannon, and the other terrific people at Four Way Books for helping usher this book into the world.

To Howard Hersh: for your belief in B and the return of K. For envisioning an alphabet's music.

Susan Morgan: so much manna from heaven you are.

And to Hideo Mabuchi: for your belief in me, unwavering. Your love, steadfast. I could not be more fortunate.

ABOUT THE AUTHOR

Cintia Santana teaches fiction and poetry workshops in Spanish, as well as literary translation courses in the Comparative Literature Department at Stanford University. Her work has appeared in *2023 Best of the Net Anthology, Best New Poets 2016* and *2020, Beloit Poetry Journal, Guernica, The Iowa Review, Kenyon Review, The Missouri Review, Narrative, Pleiades, Poetry Northwest, The Threepenny Review, West Branch,* and elsewhere. Santana's work has been supported by CantoMundo and the Djerassi Resident Artists Program. She lives in Northern California.

PUBLICATION OF THIS BOOK WAS MADE POSSIBLE
BY GRANTS AND DONATIONS. WE ARE ALSO GRATEFUL
TO THOSE INDIVIDUALS WHO PARTICIPATED IN
OUR BUILD A BOOK PROGRAM. THEY ARE:

Anonymous (14), Robert Abrams, Michael Ansara, Kathy Aponick, Jean
Ball, Sally Ball, Clayre Benzadon, Adrian Blevins, Laurel Blossom, Adam
Bohannon, Betsy Bonner, Patricia Bottomley, Lee Briccetti, Joel Brouwer, Susan
Buttenwieser, Anthony Cappo, Paul and Brandy Carlson, Dan Clarke, Mark
Conway, Elinor Cramer, Kwame Dawes, Michael Anna de Armas, John Del
Peschio, Brian Komei Dempster, Rosalynde Vas Dias, Patrick Donnelly, Lynn
Emanuel, Blas Falconer, Jennifer Franklin, John Gallaher, Reginald Gibbons,
Rebecca Kaiser Gibson, Dorothy Tapper Goldman, Julia Guez, Naomi
Guttman and Jonathan Mead, Forrest Hamer, Luke Hankins, Yona Harvey,
KT Herr, Karen Hildebrand, Carlie Hoffman, Glenna Horton, Thomas and
Autumn Howard, Catherine Hoyser, Elizabeth Jackson, Linda Susan Jackson,
Jessica Jacobs and Nickole Brown, Lee Jenkins, Elizabeth Kanell, Nancy Kassell,
Maeve Kinkead, Victoria Korth, Brett Lauer and Gretchen Scott, Howard
Levy, Owen Lewis and Susan Ennis, Margaree Little, Sara London and Dean
Albarelli, Tariq Luthun, Myra Malkin, Louise Mathias, Victoria McCoy, Lupe
Mendez, Michael and Nancy Murphy, Kimberly Nunes, Susan Okie and
Walter Weiss, Cathy McArthur Palermo, Veronica Patterson, Jill Pearlman,
Marcia and Chris Pelletiere, Sam Perkins, Susan Peters and Morgan Driscoll,
Maya Pindyck, Megan Pinto, Kevin Prufer, Martha Rhodes & Jean Brunel,
Paula Rhodes, Louise Riemer, Peter and Jill Schireson, Rob Schlegel, Yoana
Setzer, Soraya Shalforoosh, Mary Slechta, Diane Souvaine, Barbara Spark,
Catherine Stearns, Jacob Strautmann, Yerra Sugarman, Arthur Sze & Carol
Moldaw, Marjorie and Lew Tesser, Dorothy Thomas, Rushi Vyas, Martha
Webster and Robert Fuentes, Rachel Weintraub and Allston James, Abby
Wender and Rohan Weerasinghe, Monica Youn.